The Stone of Destiny

Symbol of Nationhood

David Breeze
Chief Inspector of Ancient Monuments
and
Graeme Munro
Chief Executive, Historic Scotland

HISTORIC SCOTLAND

CONTENTS

Introduction 3

THE ANGEL APPEARING TO JACOB
DEPICTED ON THE NINETEENTH-
CENTURY MUNICH STAINED GLASS,
GLASGOW CATHEDRAL.

INTRODUCTION

The Stone of Destiny is one of the most important Scottish national icons. The Stone which was formally returned to Scotland on 30 November 1996 is certainly that taken from the abbey of Scone by King Edward I of England in 1296. There can also be little doubt that Edward's men had taken the authentic Stone from the abbey, the Stone on which Scottish kings had been inaugurated for centuries. We are fortunate in possessing accounts of the inauguration of two medieval Scottish kings at Scone, Alexander III in 1249 and John Balliol in 1292. By that time, kings had been inaugurated at Scone for at least four centuries.

We then enter the realms of myth. To our ancestors, the Stone was Jacob's Pillow, the very rock on which he rested his head at Bethel when he dreamt of the ladder rising into heaven. Legend has it that the Stone was brought to Scotland by the descendants of Scota, daughter of the Pharaoh of Egypt, by way of Spain and Ireland, and transferred from an early Scots site on the west of Scotland to Scone by Kenneth MacAlpin, the king who traditionally combined the kingdoms of the Picts and the Scots in about 843.

It is not easy to disentangle fact from fiction. The Stone of Destiny is sandstone of a type found in the Perthshire area. It seems likely, therefore, that the Stone was a Pictish royal stone, adopted by the Scots when they amalgamated the two kingdoms to create Alba, centuries later becoming a British royal symbol when Scotland and England came under the same Crown in 1603.

For over 400 years perhaps, Kings of Scots were inaugurated by sitting on the Stone at Scone. For nearly 700 years Kings of England and later Kings of Great Britain and Ireland were crowned on the Stone in Westminster Abbey. Now the Stone rests again in Scotland, in Edinburgh Castle, in the Crown Room built by James VI of Scotland and James I of England, the King who united the Crowns of the two countries in 1603.

St Columba: Douglas Strachan's
stained-glass window in
St Margaret's Chapel,
Edinburgh Castle.

Iona, ancient burial place
of the Scottish kings.

CHAPTER ONE

THE INAUGURATION OF THE SCOTTISH KINGS

'*According to the custom of the nation*'

The first recorded inauguration of a king in Scotland took place on Iona in 574. Two ancient biographers of St Columba record that, following dreams in which angels appeared to him commanding him to consecrate the King, Columba ordained Aidan King of the Scots of Dalriada.

We know little about other such ceremonies in Scotland for another 500 years. By then, the kings were inaugurated at Scone in Perthshire. Scone was a Pictish royal capital when Kenneth MacAlpin, King of the Scots, also became King of the Picts about 843: according to the Scots historian John of Fordun, he killed Drosten, last King of the Picts, at Scone. Again according to Fordun, the first of Kenneth's successors to be inaugurated at Scone, probably either in 877 or 878, was Giric, a king about whom we know little. His successor, Donald II, was also inaugurated there in 889. Thereafter, although the records do not mention the inaugurations at Scone for nearly 200 years, it is fair to assume that such events took place. We certainly know that kings regularly held assemblies at Scone and that it retained its status as an important royal seat down to the reign of Malcolm III, known as Malcolm Canmore (1058–93). Malcolm's son, Alexander I, founded an abbey at Scone soon after 1120 for canons of the Augustinian Order.

After Donald II in 889, the next king recorded as being inaugurated at Scone was Lulach, who was placed on 'the royal seat' at Scone, after the death of his stepfather, Macbeth, in battle against Malcolm Canmore in 1057. His reign was brief and his successor, now Malcolm III, was also seated on 'the royal throne' at Scone following his victory over Lulach in 1058. Malcolm's descendants travelled the same path, though not always so easily: David I objected to the traditional nature of the ceremony but was persuaded to take part by his bishops. Malcolm IV was inaugurated 'according to the custom of the nation', while his brother, William the Lion, was 'lifted aloft into the royal chair' by the Bishop of St Andrews and other priests. Alexander II was 'raised to the throne' at Scone by the Bishop of St Andrews and the ceremony witnessed by the Earls of Angus, Atholl, Buchan, Fife, Lothian, Menteith and Strathearn.

On 6 July 1249 Alexander II died on the island of Kerrera near Oban and seven days later, 13 July 1249, his son, the new King of Scots, Alexander III, a boy not yet eight years old, was brought to Scone to be inaugurated. This is the first inauguration of a King of Scots to be described in detail. Remarkably, two accounts of the ceremony survive, both written by Scots historians, John of Fordun and Walter Bower, Abbot of Inchcolm, but over 100 years after the event. In the main we follow Fordun's record of the proceedings.

The boy king was accompanied to Scone by a number of the earls, barons, knights and leading churchmen of the country. At first the nobles could not agree on whether the king should be knighted before his inauguration, but eventually it was accepted that this was unnecessary. Then they:

...led Alexander, soon to be their king, up to the cross which stands in the graveyard at the east end of the church. There they set him on the royal throne, which was decked with silken cloths inwoven with gold; the Bishop of St Andrews, assisted by the rest, consecrated him king, as was meet. So the king sat down upon the royal throne – that is, the stone – while the earls and other nobles, on bended knee, strewed their garments under his feet, before the stone. Now, this stone is reverently kept in that same monastery for the consecration of Kings of Alba (Scotland); and no king was ever wont to reign in Scotland, unless he had first, on receiving the name of king, sat upon this stone at Scone, which, by the kings of old, had been appointed the capital of Alba. But lo! when all was over, a Highland Scot suddenly fell on his knees before the throne, and bowing his head, hailed the king in his mother tongue, saying these words in Gaelic:– 'Benach de Re Albanne, Alexander, MacAlexander, MacVleyham, MacHenri, MacDavid,' and, reciting it thus, he read off, even unto the end, the pedigree of the Kings of Scots. This means, in English:– 'Hail, king of Alba, Alexander, son of Alexander, son of William, son of Henry, son of David'...

THE INAUGURATION OF ALEXANDER III ON THE MOOT HILL, SCONE, ILLUSTRATED ON A LATER MEDIEVAL MANUSCRIPT. THE BARD, ON BENDED KNEE, RECITES THE KING'S ANCESTRY. THE SEAL OF SCONE ABBEY (ABOVE) DEPICTS A ROYAL INAUGURATION.

DAWN AT SCONE. THE CHAPEL ON THE MOOT HILL, BUILT IN 1624, IS WHERE CHARLES II WAS CROWNED IN 1651.

This is a most informative account of the ceremony. The king was referred to as the future king until his consecration was completed. The ceremony took place out-of-doors, more common in the past than we assume today. To enable this to happen the Stone was brought out of the abbey church, where, we are informed by another chronicler, it was kept beside the High Altar. The senior bishop, that of St Andrews, performed the ceremony which was essential to establishing the king's authority. The nobles paid homage to the king. Finally, the Gaelic bard – the King's Poet – recited the king's genealogy, thus emphasising his claim to the throne; his language is also a reminder that Scotland was formed of various peoples of different traditions and languages.

It is important, too, that this was not a coronation but an inauguration. The Scottish kings were not crowned, but given their authority through the act of sitting on the Stone. This was perceived as a point of weakness by the English kings: if their cousins in Scotland were not crowned, they alleged that they could not be full kings and were therefore inferior to the King of England. Robert the Bruce was to expend considerable effort to ensure that the inauguration was upgraded to a coronation so that the Kings of England could never again claim suzerainty.

Bower, writing 200 years later, stated that a separate 'coronation' took place before the king was seated in the chair, somewhere else, perhaps inside the abbey church, and that the king sat 'on this royal seat of stone, with his crown on his head and his sceptre in his hand, and clothed in royal purple'. Bower may be translating back to this earlier time the actions current in his day and thus introducing anachronisms to the ceremony.

THE RIVER TAY NEAR SCONE.

THE BISHOP'S PALACE, KIRKWALL, WHERE THE MAID OF NORWAY MAY HAVE DIED; THE SPIRE OF ST MAGNUS CATHEDRAL RISES UP BEHIND.

Alexander III was thus appropriately inaugurated at Scone in 1249 and reigned over his people for 36 years until, on a fateful night in mid March 1286, he was killed when he fell from his horse near Kinghorn. As his two sons and his daughter had all predeceased him, he was succeeded by his granddaughter, a child only three years old, living in Norway. The child was the daughter of Alexander's daughter, Margaret, who had married King Eric II of Norway but died in childbirth. It was this child, also Margaret, who now became the 'damsel of Scotland', though she is better known to us as the 'Maid of Norway'.

THE MAID OF NORWAY DEPICTED ON A NINETEENTH-CENTURY STAINED-GLASS WINDOW IN LERWICK TOWN HALL, SHETLAND.

Margaret's father was not keen for her to enter her inheritance immediately and in her absence Scotland was ruled by six Guardians. These Guardians and King Eric turned for advice to Margaret's nearest male relative in Britain: this man was King Edward I of England. Edward had already acquired a reputation for settling international disputes and was acknowledged as one of the most powerful kings of western Europe. He was well placed to act as an honest broker, though the Scots did not foresee how he would exploit that position to his own advantage.

Eric and Edward agreed that Margaret would marry Edward's son, Edward of Caernarfon (later Edward II), and in 1290 she sailed from Norway to Orkney, then still part of her father's kingdom. There, soon after her arrival, she died, presumably either still on her ship or in the Bishop's Palace in Kirkwall. Her body was taken back to Norway for burial.

The Guardians now sought Edward's help in choosing a successor to Margaret. There were two main claimants, John Balliol and Robert the Bruce, grandfather of the later king. Edward, asked to arbitrate, summoned all the claimants, or 'Competitors', 13 in number, to present their cases to him. The adjudication opened at Norham on the English side of the Tweed on 10 May 1291 but it was not until 17 November 1292, in the great hall of the castle at Berwick upon Tweed (then in Scotland), that Edward accepted the decision of the adjudicators and chose John Balliol as the next King of Scots. John Balliol did indeed have what was generally acknowledged to be the best claim to the throne being descended from the eldest great-granddaughter of David I. The claim of Robert the Bruce was based on the fact that, while he was descended from her younger sister, he was one generation closer to David I and descended through only one female, unlike Balliol whose claim passed through two females.

THE SEAL OF JOHN BALLIOL.

8

THE REMAINS OF THE CASTLE AT
BERWICK UPON TWEED, WHERE
EDWARD I OF ENGLAND DECLARED JOHN
BALLIOL KING OF SCOTS IN 1292.

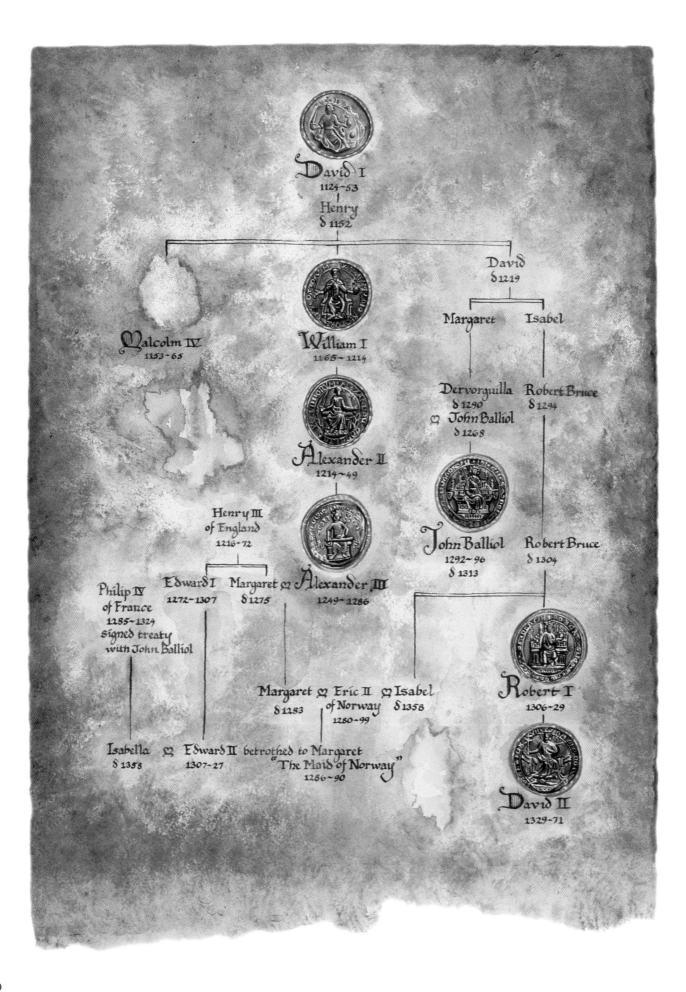

David I
1124-53

Henry
δ 1152

Malcolm IV
1153-65

William I
1165-1214

Alexander II
1214-49

David
δ 1219

Margaret   Isabel

Dervorguilla   Robert Bruce
δ 1290   δ 1294
∞ John Balliol
δ 1268

John Balliol   Robert Bruce
1292-96   δ 1304
δ 1313

Henry III
of England
1216-72

Edward I   Margaret ∞ Alexander III
1272-1307   δ1275   1249-1286

Philip IV
of France
1285-1324
signed treaty
with John Balliol

Margaret ∞ Eric II ∞ Isabel
δ 1283   of Norway   δ 1358
1280-99

Robert I
1306-29

Isabella ∞ Edward II betrothed to Margaret
δ 1358   1307-27   "The Maid of Norway"
                              1286-90

David II
1329-71

Following the decision, King John proceeded to Scone to sit upon the Stone. John of Fordun is brief on the occasion: 'on the last day of November 1292, this John de Balliol was made king at Scone; and having been set there on the royal throne, as is the custom, he was promoted in due manner'. William Rishanger in his *Chronicles and Annals*, written about 1327, offers a little more: 'John de Balliol, on the following feast of St Andrew, placed upon the regal stone, which Jacob placed under his head when he went from Beersheba to Haran, was solemnly crowned in the church of the canons regular at Scone'. Walter of Guisborough gives the most detailed account: 'on St Andrew's Day John Balliol was made King of Scotland according to the Scottish custom... In the Coronation Chair future kings were set, according to the custom, as the place of their coronation. The placing of the new sovereign in this seat belonged by hereditary right to the Earl of Fife. The King then took the oath that he would protect Holy Mother Church, and his subjects, by ruling justly; and that he would establish good laws and continue the customs and institutions of the nation as long as he lived. When Balliol had been placed upon the Stone, the solemn rites of mass were begun and completed, and he also remained seated upon it during the elevation of the Sacred Host.' As the Earl of Fife was a child at the time, he did not place the king in the royal seat; the task was delegated to Sir John de St John, an official of King Edward. It seems that the ceremony took place inside the abbey church, unlike the inauguration of Alexander III.

This was to be the last time that a King of Scots sat on the royal Stone at Scone. There were to be other coronations at Scone, including that of Charles II in 1651, but none on the Stone, which by then lay over 400 miles away in Westminster Abbey. However, a Scots king was to sit on the Stone again: in 1603 James VI became James I of England and on 25 July was crowned at Westminster Abbey, sitting in the Coronation Chair which held the Stone of Destiny.

EDWARD I OF ENGLAND RECEIVES THE HOMAGE OF JOHN BALLIOL.

THE SCOTTISH ROYAL LINE
SHOWING LINKS WITH ENGLAND
AND NORWAY.

11

CHAPTER TWO

THE STONE IN WESTERN EUROPEAN TRADITION

'Consecrated on a Sunday'

The use of stone as part of an act of investiture is of great antiquity. In Scotland there were once several examples of footprints carved out of rock surfaces which, it is believed, were used in such symbolic acts. The best known footprints are on the hilltop of Dunadd in Argyll. The better preserved is 280 mm (11 in) long, nearly 110 mm (4½ in) wide and 90 mm (3½ in) across at the heel, so large that it would fit a foot clothed in a shoe or boot.

Dunadd was one of the strongholds of the kingdom of Dalriada established by the Scots following the traditional date of their immigration from Ireland in about 500. Dunadd therefore would have been a most appropriate place for an investiture ceremony. Interestingly, the rock into which the footprint was cut also contains other symbols: an inscription in ogham script and a boar, thought by some to be Pictish.

Another rock footprint – or rather footprints for there are two – is cut into a stone beside the causeway leading across the lochan to the prehistoric settlement at Clickhimin in Shetland. Clickhimin was occupied from about 1000 BC to AD 500 but within that period the date of the cutting of the footprints is not known.

Other footprints survive at Southend in Argyll, at Burwick in South Ronaldsay in Orkney, and formerly existed at Yell, in Shetland, and in Angus, where two examples have been recorded. Foot-marked rocks are also known in Ireland and in France.

The act of a king or chief standing on a special stone to be invested can be seen as symbolic of a relationship with an object of great antiquity – rock – with nature, and also with the land from which his people earned their food. It is but a short step to remove a piece of such rock and make it into an object on which a king sat to be invested. Such carved stones are recorded not only in Scotland but also in England and Ireland.

DUNADD (ABOVE LEFT) RISES ABOVE CRINAN MOSS.

(INSET) A FOOTPRINT IN THE ROCK ON THE SUMMIT OF DUNADD.

THE STONE AT KINGSTON UPON THAMES, ENGLAND.

THE STONE FOOTPRINTS AT CLICKHIMIN, SHETLAND.

We are so used to the relationship between the English coronation and Westminster Abbey that it comes as something of a surprise to discover that earlier English kings were crowned elsewhere. At least seven English kings of the West Saxon dynasty were crowned at Kingston upon Thames: its name, alas, does not derive from 'king's stone', but from 'king's town'.

Edward the Elder, son of Alfred the Great, was the first king to hold his coronation at Kingston, in 900, where he was crowned by the Archbishop of Canterbury. His son and several successors down to Ethelred the Unready in 979 were also crowned there.

'He was consecrated on a Sunday, a fortnight after Easter, and at his consecration were two archbishops and ten diocesan bishops.' Ethelred's son, Edmund Ironside, may have been the last king to have been crowned at Kingston, in 1016.

It is not clear where the Saxon kings were crowned, but it was probably in the town's church. The large sandstone block which still sits outside the church in the market-place is said to be the stone on which they sat to receive their crown. However, it is possible that the crowning took place within the church with the king later sitting on the stone outside to be presented to the people.

SCONE PALACE OVERLOOKING
THE RIVER TAY.

THE STONE
IDENTIFIED AS THE
LIA FAIL AT TARA,
COUNTY MEATH,
IRELAND. THE
STONE WAS MOVED
FROM NEARBY IN
1798 AND NOW
STANDS ON THE
MOUND WITHIN THE
EARTHWORK KNOWN
AS CORMAC'S
HOUSE.

There is an interesting coincidence between the positions of Scone and Kingston: both lie at the highest tidal point on the rivers on which they sit. It has been suggested that this location is symbolic. Here fresh water and salt water met: did the point where the sweet, fresh water repelled the salt symbolise the power of life over death?

Several stone chairs have been recorded in Ireland. One formerly stood at Tullaghoge in County Tyrone. Here the O'Neills were inaugurated since the time of St Columba, if we believe tradition. As part of the ceremony, the new lord had a slipper or sandal placed on his foot by the hereditary lawgiver, an act which reminds us of the foot-marked stone at Dunadd. The stone chair was smashed by Lord Mountjoy in 1602 after he put down the rebellion of the O'Neills. The O'Neills had another chair at Castlereagh near Belfast. Here the junior branch of the family had their chief inaugurated. This chair, in turn, was thrown down and neglected during the reign of James VI and I: it is now in the Ulster Museum, Belfast.

Another Irish stone, the Coronation Stone of the Kings of Munster, stood on the Rock of Cashel, while the *Lia Fail*, the 'fatal chair', at Tara held a special place in Irish tradition and mythology for it was believed that about 500 the original stone from here was lent to Fergus MacErc to allow him to be inaugurated King of the Scots of Dalriada.

Stone chairs are recorded elsewhere in Europe. The medieval Dukes of Carinthia in Austria were inaugurated at Zollfeld on a throne created out of Roman masonry, and the Kings of Sweden on a stone chair at Uppsala.

Sometimes stone chairs or thrones were specially made for monarchs. The tradition seems to have started with the Byzantine emperors in Constantinople, and was adopted by the Holy Roman Emperors in the west, whose most famous surviving throne, named after the first Holy Roman Emperor, Charlemagne, still sits in his cathedral at Aachen in Germany. This throne was actually made for the coronation of Otto I in 936 and was used until 1531, when the ceremony was transferred to Frankfurt.

MYTH AND SYMBOLISM

*'If destiny deceives not, the Scots will reign 'tis said
in that same place where the Stone has been laid'*

In the year 297, a Roman writer recorded that people from Ireland raided the Roman empire. Twenty years later, these people were named Scoti or Scotti. They continued to trouble the Romans for the next century. According to tradition, it was about 500, a century after Britain was cut off from the Roman empire, that the Scotti under their leader, Fergus MacErc, conquered Argyll. Here they founded a kingdom which, for a time, spread over both sides of the North Channel between Scotland and Ireland.

The legend of the arrival of the Scots was later embroidered and linked to events of even greater antiquity. We first hear the story of Scota in the eleventh century, perhaps even later. According to this tale, amongst the army of the Egyptians which pursued the Israelites through the Red Sea was a Scythian nobleman. He, however, did not enter the Red Sea but was expelled from Egypt by the survivors because they feared that he might take over their kingdom. The Scythian, with his wife Scota, daughter of the Pharaoh of Egypt, wandered through Africa and crossed into Spain at the Pillars of Hercules. Some of their descendants moved on to Ireland and thence Argyll: the arrival in Ireland was dated to 1002 years after the Egyptians had been drowned in the Red Sea!

Our first certain record of the entry of the Stone to this tradition is in the year 1301. In that year Scottish and English representatives were pleading their respective cases before the Pope in Rome. We possess both the draft prepared by the Scots lawyer, Baldred Bisset, and his team of procurators and his own amended version. His own version reads:

...the daughter of Pharaoh, King of Egypt, went to Ireland with an armed following and a large fleet. Afterwards, a large number of Hibernians (i.e. Irish) having joined her band, she sailed to Scotland, taking with her the royal seat, which the King of England has forcibly carried off. She overcame and destroyed the Picts and took possession of their kingdom, and from this Scota the Scots and Scotia are named.

It is clear, by comparing this passage with the draft, that Baldred introduced the Stone into the case which he also amended by having Scota lead the army not only into Ireland but also to Scotland. The reason was presumably to try to improve his argument. The English case was based upon the tradition that their king was descended from the elder son of Brutus, after whom Britain was named, while the Scots were descended from a younger son. In such a plea, a little elaboration is not surprising!

A song about the Stone was composed in England, probably shortly after the death of Edward I in 1307. In this it is stated that Scota, Pharaoh's daughter, brought the Stone directly from Egypt to Scotland, to a place close to Scone. Twenty years later William de Rishanger offered further elaboration when he wrote that John Balliol sat on 'the royal stone which Jacob placed under his head when he was going from Beersheba to Haran'.

THE ARRIVAL OF SCOTA IN SCOTLAND AS PORTRAYED BY A MEDIEVAL ARTIST IN WALTER BOWER'S *SCOTICHRONICON*.

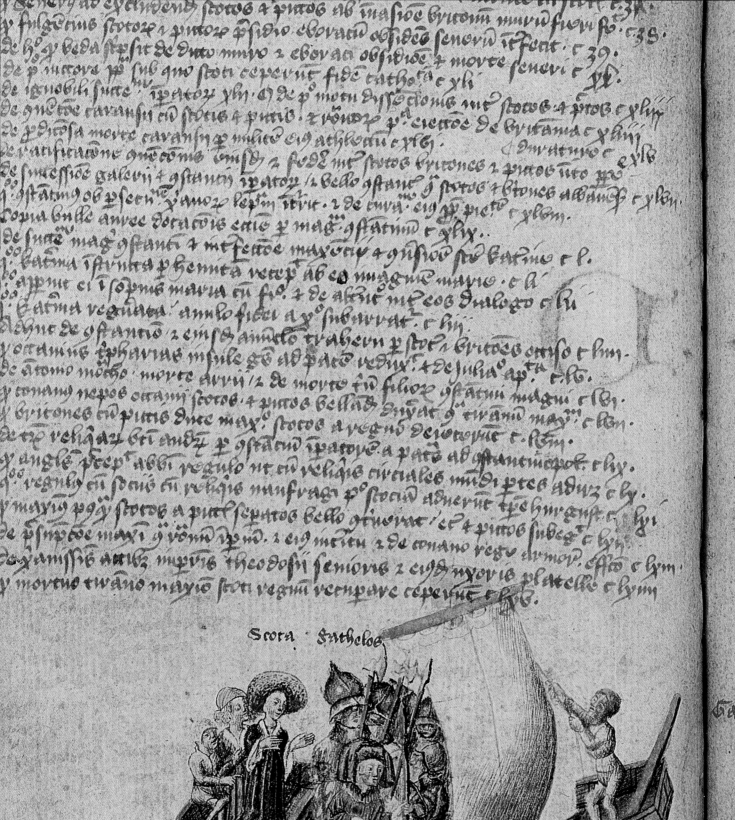

Scota · Gatheloe

John of Fordun in his *Scotichronicon*, written in the mid 14th century but drawing on earlier sources, provided the most detailed account of the traditional conquest of Argyll by the Scots. He introduces us to Simon Brec, son of a King of Spain and descendant of Scota. According to Fordun, Simon Brec was sent by his father from Spain to Ireland with 'a marble throne of very ancient workmanship, carved by a careful craftsman, on which the kings of the Scottish people in Spain used to sit. ... He placed the aforesaid stone, that is the throne, in a place in his kingdom of some height which was called Tara.' Fordun added that one tradition was that the seat was brought from Egypt to Spain, but another:

...that Simon Brec let down anchors from his ship and secured them in the sea near the Irish coast. When he was forced by adverse winds to pull them up again from the stormy seas, he only just managed to do so with the utmost possible effort, and along with the anchors he raised from the depths of the seas and pulled into the ship a block of marble cut in the shape of a chair. So he accepted this stone as a precious gift bestowed on him by the gods and as a sure omen that he would be king. ... He also received a prophecy about it from his gods...that in future in whatsoever kingdom or lordship they found the Stone after it had been forcibly removed from them through the power of their enemies, the prophets bade them regard it as certain that they and their

DUNSTAFFNAGE CASTLE, NEAR OBAN.

JACOB RESTS HIS HEAD ON THE STONE PILLOW: A DETAIL FROM THE STAINED-GLASS WINDOW IN GLASGOW CATHEDRAL.

descendants would reign thereafter in that same place. This has been expressed in prophetic verse as follows:

If destiny deceives not, the Scots will reign 'tis said in that same place where the Stone has been laid.

Sir Walter Scott was later to render this as:

Unless the Fates are faithless found
And prophets' voice be vain,
Where'er this monument is found
The Scottish race shall reign.

As the Scotti first settled in Argyll, it is not difficult to see how a link was then made with Iona, the foremost Christian site in the west of Scotland. This appears to have been first made by Andrew de Wyntoun, writing in the early 1400s, who stated that the Stone was first placed at Iona and only later transferred to Scone. Iona's claim to be the original home of the Stone was strengthened by a combination of separate events. The *Pictish Chronicle* recorded that in 849 Kenneth MacAlpin transferred the relics of St Columba from Iona to a church which he built at Dunkeld. Earlier, Columba's biographers had stated that the saint rested his head on a stone pillow. It was a simple next step to bring all together and assume that the Stone was brought from Iona and that it was the Pillow of Jacob. Another legend links the Stone with Dunstaffnage, near Oban: John Monipennie writing in the late sixteenth century stated that 'the kings of Scotland in old times (were) crowned' at Dunstaffnage and here also 'the marble fatal chair remained more than one thousand years'.

Thus was created the story of the Stone, woven round traditions stretching over centuries and all helping to create a powerful symbol.

THE REMOVAL OF THE STONE FROM SCOTLAND

'To London led'

The death of Alexander III at Kinghorn in 1286 marked the end of an epoch in Scottish history. He had reigned for 36 years and his two immediate predecessors, Alexander II and William I, for 35 years and 49 years respectively. Scotland's southern border had been established more or less on its present line and Alexander III had taken a major step to recover lands lost to the Vikings centuries before. Three years after the Battle of Largs in 1263, by the Treaty of Perth, Norway ceded the Hebrides and the Isle of Man to Scotland; it would be another 200 years before Orkney and Shetland would come under the Scottish Crown. During the two centuries prior to the death of Alexander III Scotland had enjoyed long periods of relative peace and stability. Although geographically remote from the main power centres of continental Europe, it nevertheless enjoyed many of the economic and cultural fruits of what is often called the twelfth-century Renaissance.

It was this relatively sophisticated and evolving society which faltered after the death of Alexander III. The lack of a strong heir to the throne provided scope for external intervention in Scottish affairs.

King Edward I of England utilised the vacuum in the Scottish kingdom to enforce his view that the King of Scots was his feudal vassal. In the past, Kings of Scots had

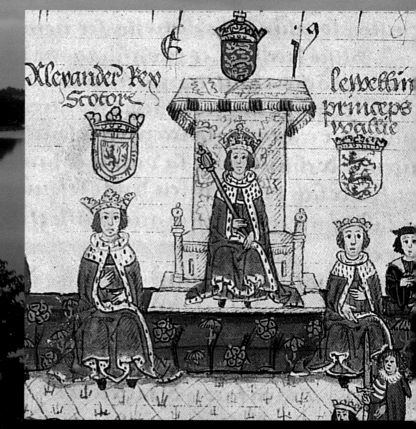

EDWARD I OF ENGLAND, SEATED ON HIS CANOPIED THRONE, IS FLANKED BY ALEXANDER III OF SCOTLAND AND LLYWELYN, PRINCE OF WALES.

given homage to Kings of England, but only for their estates south of the Border. They had carefully resisted all attempts to extend that homage to their Scottish kingdom, though occasionally they had been forced to succumb. As recently as 1278 Alexander III had insisted to Edward I that 'no-one has a right to homage for my kingdom of Scotland save God alone, and I hold it only of God'

As part of the price for his role as adjudicator of the claims of the 13 Competitors for the throne of Scotland, Edward extracted from the claimants recognition of his position as overlord, though, to be fair to Edward, he may have done this as a guarantee that his judgement could be enforced. He now insisted that King John also pay homage. This was done immediately after the decision at Berwick, and again after the King's inauguration at Scone in 1292 when King John, accompanied by many Scots nobles, travelled south into England to swear fealty to Edward at Newcastle in December.

To understand the background to the removal of the Stone of Destiny it is necessary to know a little about the character of Edward I. Edward possessed all the attributes of a great medieval king, offering strong and energetic but autocratic leadership tempered by care for the welfare of his people. Yet his autocracy could tip over into arrogance, violence and cruelty, especially when thwarted, while concern for his legal rights sometimes led to an inflexible and narrow insistence on the letter rather than the spirit of the law, which in Scotland in the long run worked to his disadvantage. Edward had learnt military leadership in the English civil war of the 1260s, when still a prince, and, following victory, the arts of peace though after initially displaying a vengeful attitude to his father's

peaceful to allow him to go on a Crusade. In 1272, when still returning from the Holy Land, Edward succeeded his father as King of England, Lord of Ireland and Duke of Aquitaine. He not only had extensive lands, but pretensions to overlordship of the whole of the British Isles. When Llywelyn, Prince of Wales, refused homage, Edward invaded and conquered his principality, reducing its size. Edward's settlement was overthrown when Llywelyn supported his brother David's rebellion in 1282. Llywelyn was killed in a skirmish, David executed and Wales 'annexed to the crown of England'. In 1290 he expelled the Jews from England. His intervention in Scotland has to be seen in the light of this aggressive pursuit of his ambitions.

For nearly four years after 1292 King John vainly tried to resist the increasing pressure placed on him by Edward. The crucial act of defiance occurred in the summer of 1294. Edward, faced with a war against France, summoned King John, 10 Scottish earls and 16 barons for service in his army. The Scots defied the summons, arranged a treaty with the French (this is often considered to be the beginning of the Auld Alliance, though France and Scotland had cooperated before) and prepared to resist. The Treaty was ratified by the French in 1295 and by the Scottish Parliament, sitting in Dunfermline,

Retribution was swift. On 28 March the English army crossed the border at Coldstream and two days later Berwick, then the most important Scottish royal burgh and port, was sacked and its inhabitants massacred on the orders of Edward. The next month the Scots army was signally defeated at Dunbar. In July, at a ceremony at Montrose clearly designed to humiliate, King John was stripped of his crown, sceptre and ring and the royal arms from his surcoat, leading to his subsequent nickname: 'Toom Tabard' or empty coat – King Nobody.

King John was taken south and imprisoned in the Tower of London. To London were also transported the Scottish regalia (the crown, sceptre, sword, ring and royal robe), the royal records (a memorandum of 1323 records 65 containers of documents), jewellery, plate and relics, including the Scots' fragment of the True Cross, known as the Black Rood (cross) of St Margaret. These were lodged in the Palace of Westminster. Edward also seized the Stone of Destiny.

In August 1296, while on his way from Dundee to St Andrews via Perth, Edward sent a force to Scone to take the Stone. A later report states that it was lodged in Edinburgh Castle, but this is not certain. We do know that it was sent south the following month. Contemporaries were in no doubt as to what was intended by this symbolic act. Edward saw it as a sign of victory, a symbol that Scotland had been conquered and resigned by Balliol into his hands. His English subjects recognised this and sang of his triumph:

The Azure of the Balliol

*Their kings' seat of Scone
is driven over down,
to London led.*

*I'll tell you truly what the Stone of Scotland is...
Now Edward King of England has taken it,
By the grace of Jesus and by hard fighting.
To Saint Edward has he given it.*

That the Stone returned to Scotland in 1996 is certainly the one removed in 1296 is beyond serious doubt. There will, however, probably always be speculation as to whether Edward I took the 'real' Stone of Scone south in 1296. It has been argued that the Abbot of Scone would have been likely to have hidden the Stone following Edward's invasion of Scotland. Yet, Edward was able to lay hands on the crown, sceptre and ring and the Black Rood of St Margaret, all of which could have been more easily secreted away. If the real Stone had been hidden, it is almost inconceivable that it would not have been

produced for the coronation of Robert the Bruce only ten years later, in 1306, especially since Bishop Wishart of Glasgow was able to produce appropriate robes and vestments for the occasion and even a banner bearing the arms of the last king. Right up to the end of his reign Bruce was keen to secure the return of the Stone to Scotland. Finally, at least one of Edward's officers, as well as the Bishop of Durham, had been present at the inauguration of King John and could presumably have verified that the Stone taken by Edward was genuine.

Exactly how the Stone was taken south is not recorded, though there is some evidence that it was taken by road. It has been suggested that the iron rings and staples, at each end of the Stone, were embedded in it prior to its removal from Scotland expressly to aid its transportation, but modern scientific analysis of the Stone makes this unlikely.

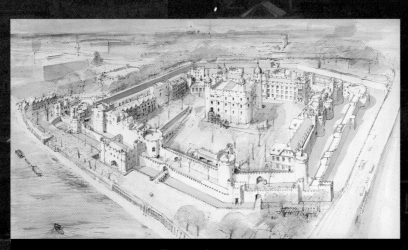

AN IMPRESSION OF THE TOWER OF LONDON AS IT MIGHT HAVE LOOKED

CHAPTER FIVE

700 YEARS ABSENCE

'To Saint Edward has he given it'

In 1296 Edward was 57 years old. In an age when life expectancy was shorter than today, and with the deaths in 1290 of his Queen, Eleanor, and in 1292 of his chancellor, Burnell, who had both been good influences on him, Edward may well have been contemplating his own mortality and seeking to associate himself with his saintly predecessor, with whom he shared a name but little else.

The Scottish crown and the sceptre and the Stone were presented to Westminster Abbey in June 1297 (another crown was taken from Balliol before he left England in 1299 and presented to Canterbury Cathedral). King Edward determined that the Stone should be suitably housed and ordered the making of a special bronze chair. However, in July 1297 work on the chair was halted, probably owing to Edward's financial difficulties, and it was replaced by a gilt wood version which was completed by March 1300. This chair, made by Walter of Durham, is the earliest surviving example of a new style of throne favoured by the kings of western Europe. The chair can be seen as a trophy case for the Stone.

In placing the Stone at Westminster Abbey with the Crown of Arthur seized by Edward from the Welsh and the fragments of the True Cross, Edward brought together the symbols which he considered supported his claim to overlordship of the whole of Britain. These objects not only underlined his conquests of Wales and Scotland but emphasised Biblical support for his position. After all, when Jacob had arisen from his pillow and climbed the ladder to heaven, he was promised the land on which he lay. The Stone was thus linked to a promise of territory and both Edward and his Scottish foes understood this.

No matter how the Stone was borne south, Edward I decided to place it in the chapel within Westminster Abbey dedicated to St Edward the Confessor. Edward was both a sincerely religious man and also extremely devoted to the memory of his father, Henry III, who had rebuilt Westminster Abbey. Thus the choice of the abbey for trophies of war is not surprising.

THE STONE OF DESTINY IN THE CORONATION CHAIR, WESTMINSTER ABBEY (LEFT), PRIOR TO ITS RETURN TO SCOTLAND.

THE STATUE OF
WILLIAM WALLACE NEAR
DRYBURGH ABBEY.

Rishanger's *Chronicles and Annals* record that in 1296 Edward had ordered the removal of the 'Stone, on which, as has been said, the Kings of the Scots were wont to be placed at their coronation .... as a sign that the kingdom had been conquered and resigned'. If Edward thought he had conquered Scotland, he was soon proved wrong. The uprising with which William Wallace's name will forever be associated broke out in May 1297 and he won his famous victory at Stirling Bridge in September of that year. Although this uprising was eventually crushed and Wallace executed, new uprisings occurred, culminating with the seizure of the throne by

Bruce's first significant act after murdering John Comyn at Dumfries in February was to go to Scone. Here on 25 March every effort was made to follow the traditional style of inauguration. The ceremony was witnessed by five earls, four bishops and 'the people of the land'. The Earl of Fife, who had the role of leading the King to the Stone, was captive in England, so his aunt, Isabel, Countess of Buchan, took his place. However, there was now no Stone so Bruce was placed on a throne. It is not known where the inauguration took place. It seems probable that the abbey church was the location for Edward I was so angry that he

Two days later, on Palm Sunday, there was a high mass for the new king in the abbey church and on one if not both these occasions a simple gold crown, newly made, was placed on King Robert's head. The new crown did not survive long in Scotland for it was captured from Bruce after his defeat at the Battle of Methven later that year. Edward set off north again on what proved to be his last campaign against the Scots. Indeed, he never reached Scotland; he died at Burgh-by-Sands, on the southern shore of the Solway Firth and in sight of Scotland. In his own day he was nicknamed 'Edward Longshanks', a reference to his height. The nickname 'Hammer of the Scots' came centuries later when England and Scotland

were again at war and the English wished to use Edward as a role-model for propaganda and morale-boosting purposes.

Whether Edward deserves to be remembered as the Hammer of the Scots is arguable. At the time of his death Bruce had been crowned king and the English Exchequer sorely depleted by the campaigns against Scotland. Edward I's body was brought back from Burgh-by-Sands to London where he was buried in the chapel of Edward the Confessor, only feet away from the Stone of Destiny. He had captured one of the most potent symbols of Scottish nationhood but had failed in his mission to destroy Scotland's existence as a distinct nation.

The loss of the symbolic Stone did not deter the Scots from their goal of seeking to establish in the eyes of the Papacy and international opinion their right to crown their own kings. In 1299 an embassy of clergy had been sent to Rome seeking the Pope's intercession to prevent Edward I absorbing Scotland. Following their victory at Bannockburn in 1314, the Scots were not content to rest on their *de facto* independence but sought to have it recognised. The Declaration of Arbroath of 1320 was a direct appeal to the Pope to lift the excommunication on Robert the Bruce (for his murder of Comyn). In this specific purpose it failed but the Declaration contains a stirring assertion of Scottish nationhood:

It is not for honours, nor glory nor riches that we fight but for freedom alone which no good man puts down but with his life. So long as one hundred of us remain alive we shall not submit to English domination.

Bruce's title to the throne was recognised by the Pope in 1324. Following 14 years of desultory war after the clinching victory of Bannockburn, a peace treaty was agreed between England and Scotland in Edinburgh in March 1328. The treaty was ratified by the English Parliament the following year at Northampton. The Scots paid £20,000 (possibly in war damages for their incursions into northern England over a 20-year period) while the independence of Scotland 'separate in all things from the Kingdom of England' was recognised.

This recognition paved the way for what the Scots had long craved. In 1329 the Pope permitted the anointing of the Kings of Scots at their enthronement. In medieval terms this was the equivalent of admission to the United Nations today and set the seal on international recognition of Scotland's status. By June 1329 Bruce was dead but, unlike Edward, he had achieved his primary aims. He was buried in the Abbey of Dunfermline and his son, David II, was duly anointed King of Scots.

Under the Treaty of Edinburgh of 1328 there was specific agreement to return to Scotland the Black Rood of St Margaret and certain documents taken south with the Stone in 1296. The Treaty itself is silent on the regalia and the Stone. No more is heard of the regalia, but there seems to have been an understanding about the return of the Stone. The English Parliament, sitting at Northampton, issued two edicts relating to the Stone. The first required the Abbot of Westminster to hand it over to the Sheriffs of London. The second ordered the Sheriffs to transport the Stone to the north of England and hand it over to Queen Isabel who was about to enter negotiations with the Scots over the question of lands privately held by Englishmen in Scotland prior to the wars and declared forfeit by Robert the Bruce. The Queen had effectively displaced the weak Edward II as the power in the land and it seems that she intended to use the Stone as a bargaining counter.

It is far from clear that the Scots would have responded to this negotiating ploy in quite the way which the English hoped. By this time they had achieved the independence and recognition for which they had fought. In any case, the Scots' attitude to these putative negotiations was never to be tested. The Abbot of Westminster, in a classic stalling manoeuvre, declared that it was not for Parliament to instruct him to hand over the Stone which had been given to the Abbey by the late King Edward. He argued that he required clarification of the decision and refused to

hand over the Stone. The Sheriffs of London simply reported the Abbot's recalcitrance. They were probably relieved to be able to do so since the London mob was demonstrating against the return of the Stone of Scotland. The moment passed and the Stone remained in London.

The Black Rood was duly returned to Scotland as promised. The Scots appear to have been as much upset by the theft of this sacred relic in 1296 as by the removal of the Stone and other symbols of temporal power. By a twist of fate, the Scots lost the Black Rood again in 1346, having borne it with them into battle at Neville's Cross during David II's ill-fated incursion into northern England.

The possibility of the Stone's return to Scotland arose again briefly later in the fourteenth century. David II was wounded at Neville's Cross and taken captive to be held prisoner in England for a decade. He was ransomed in 1356, but the burden of repayment led to significantly higher taxation. In 1363 the nobility rebelled. In negotiations at Westminster later that year Edward III of England offered more favourable terms for the repayment of the ransom in exchange for the Scottish throne passing to Edward, or one of his sons, on David's death. David II took these proposals to the Scottish Parliament, sitting at Scone, who threw them out. Had Edward succeeded in his attempt to achieve by diplomacy what his father and grandfather had failed to bring about by war, he had intended to bring the Stone back to Scotland.

Between the mid fourteenth and the nineteenth century there were few events which bear directly on the history of the Stone. Perhaps the most significant event occurred in 1603 when, on the death of Queen Elizabeth I, James VI of Scotland also became King James I of England. When he went south he was crowned in Westminster Abbey, on the Stone on which his ancestors had been inaugurated more than 300 years previously. For many commentators, then and since, this is seen as bearing out the prophecy that Scots would reign wherever the Stone lay.

KING JAMES VI AND I CROWNED AND SEATED ON HIS ENGLISH THRONE.

No concerted effort appears to have been made to have the Stone restored to Scotland before 1924 when a Bill with that as its aim was introduced in Parliament by David Kirkwood

DAVID KIRKWOOD.

MP and was given a First Reading by 201 votes to 171 on 15 July. Among those voting against were Stanley Baldwin, Neville Chamberlain and Anthony Eden. Although the Prime Minister of the day, Ramsay Macdonald, was a Scot, he declined to support the further progress of the Bill on the grounds that there were other legislative priorities and that he wished to keep the autumn session of Parliament short.

On Christmas Day 1950 four Scottish students (Ian Hamilton, Kay Matheson, Alan Stuart and Gavin Vernon) succeeded in removing the Stone from Westminster Abbey. They broke into the Abbey by forcing the Poet's Corner door. They then pulled the Stone from the Coronation Chair and dragged it on a coat from the Abbey to a Ford Anglia car waiting in Palace Yard. Until recently it has been widely believed that the Stone was broken at this time, but at least one of the former students now claims that the Stone was already broken when they took it from the Coronation Chair: there was indeed a crack across the Stone, clear in earlier photographs. The Stone, in two parts, was brought north. A major hunt was mounted but the Stone was not tracked down by the police.

Three months later, on 11 April, the Stone was placed in Arbroath Abbey. The *Daily Herald* reported that on 12 April there had been a steady stream of visitors to Arbroath Abbey and the custodian, Mr James Wishart, had cancelled his day off! By then, however, the Stone was already on its way back to Westminster Abbey,

but it was to be nearly a year before it went back on display in the Coronation Chair. Recently released papers show that the Secretary of State for Scotland, Hector McNeil, put a paper to his Labour Cabinet colleagues canvassing three options: (1) to leave the Stone in Westminster Abbey; (2) to return it to Scotland for custody between Coronations; and (3) to arrange for it to be displayed in the capital cities of the Commonwealth, beginning with Edinburgh. It is fairly clear that Hector McNeil favoured the second option but was unable to persuade the Cabinet, which decided on 7 May to postpone for at least a year a decision on what advice to give King George VI on the future of the Stone. In a debate in the House of Lords on 9 May, seven peers spoke in favour of returning the Stone to Scotland, with only one opposing and two adopting a neutral stance. The Government spokesman indicated that the issue was under consideration. Later that month the General Assembly of the Church of Scotland declined to endorse a report from its Church and Nation Committee which, while condemning the removal of the Stone from Westminster, argued that 'a reasonable and acceptable solution would be found if the responsible authorities should decide to entrust the guardianship of the Stone to Scottish hands on Scottish soil'. Over the

THREE OF THE STUDENTS WHO REMOVED THE STONE IN 1950.

summer and autumn months the Dean of Westminster continued to lobby the Government in private for a decision in favour of Westminster. In October there was a change of Government and by then King George VI was ill. The incoming Government, with Winston Churchill as Prime Minister, resolved at a Cabinet meeting early in February 1952 to recommend that the Stone be kept at Westminster and the agreement of the Leader of the Opposition, Clement Attlee, was obtained in advance of the announcement to Parliament on 26 February 1952 by the Prime Minister:

For over 650 years the Stone has been in Westminster Abbey and, from its use at successive Coronations it has a historic significance for all countries in the Commonwealth. With the approval of Her Majesty's Government, the Stone has been restored to its traditional place.

For the time being the arguments in favour of retention at Westminster Abbey had won and the Stone was put back on display in the Coronation Chair, without ceremony. It was, however, significant that the possibility of a return to Scotland between Coronations had been seriously entertained at the highest political level.

Although the taking of the Stone in 1950 was an illegal act, none of the perpetrators was prosecuted. The incident ensured that many more twentieth-century Scots were aware of its history, and indeed of its very existence, than before. Many who felt unhappy about the way in which the Stone had been taken from Westminster nonetheless had sympathy with the historical arguments for an eventual return of the Stone to Scotland.

THE RETURN OF THE STONE

'The recovery of this ancient symbol cannot but strengthen the proud distinctiveness of the people of Scotland'

In February 1996 a major exhibition was held in Stirling Castle to mark the 700th anniversary of the Auld Alliance between Scotland and France. The exhibition covered several centuries and contained many valuable documents on loan from the National Archives of France, including the French version of the Treaty of Alliance between Scotland and France (and Norway). It was both fascinating and moving for many Scots to be able to see this ancient document which provided the visible evidence of the Auld Alliance. For those who saw it, this exhibition brought the events of 1296 dramatically to life. Nobody foresaw that before the year was out there would be an even greater and more dramatic event linked to Scotland's past.

The ratification of the treaty of mutual support between Scotland and France in February 1296 was followed immediately by Edward I's invasion of Scotland and the seizure of the Stone of Destiny. There was thus another important anniversary in 1996. Attempts earlier this century to return the Stone to Scotland by persuasion or by direct action (1950 and 1974, when a student had tried to take the Stone) had failed but all had provoked a public debate. There was no such debate in the early months of 1996, despite the significance of the anniversary.

There had, therefore, been no hint of what was to come when the Prime Minister rose to his feet in the House of Commons on 3 July 1996 to make a statement about the Stone of Destiny:

The Stone of Destiny is the most ancient symbol of Scottish kingship. It was used in the coronation of Scottish Kings until the end of the 13th century. Exactly 700 years ago, in 1296, King Edward I brought it from Scotland and housed it in Westminster Abbey. The Stone remains the property of the Crown. I wish to inform the House that, on the advice of Her Majesty's Ministers, The Queen has agreed that the Stone should be returned to Scotland. The Stone will, of course, be taken to Westminster Abbey to play its traditional role in the coronation ceremonies of future sovereigns of the United Kingdom.

The Stone of Destiny holds a special place in the hearts of Scots. On this, the 700th anniversary of its removal from Scotland, it is appropriate to return it to its historic homeland. I am sure that the House would wish to be assured that the Stone will be placed in an appropriate setting in Scotland. The Government will be consulting Scottish and Church opinion about that. The Stone might be displayed in Edinburgh Castle alongside the Honours of Scotland, Europe's oldest crown jewels. Alternatively, it might be appropriate to place it in St Margaret's Chapel inside the Castle or in St Giles' Cathedral. There may be other options.

Once those consultations have been completed, the necessary arrangements will be made and the Stone will be installed with due dignity in Scotland.

ELIZABETH THE SE...
Realms and Territories...
GREETING! WHEREAS...
of the Crown; AND WHERE...
and of Their Other Realms an...
AND WHEREAS the said Ston...
estminster, otherwise known as...
s late Majesty George the Third on the...
s in office were appointed to safeguard, rep...
Us that it is appropriate that the said St...
KNOW·YE that We, in consideration of cir...
sure, have nominated, constituted and ordained ou...
First) Our Trusty and Well-beloved Counsellor Michael ...
eat Seal of Scotland, (Second) Our Right Trusty and Right...
t of Our Most Ancient and Most Noble Order of the Thistle...
ellor Donald Sage Mackay, Lord Mackay of Drumadoon, On...
d Well-beloved Counsellor Donald MacArthur Ross commonly...
cessors as aforementioned to guard the said Stone of Scone on...
y to them or any two of them-(Firstly) of making appropriate arrangement...
vereigns of the United Kingdom of Great Britain and Northern Ireland and...
y, Our said Successors be set upon the said Stone of Scone; (Secondly) of...
riate to them for the custody due to the said Stone of Scone in Our Castle of Edinburgh or in...
cotland as seems suitable to Us to constitute from time to time and when transporting the said...
hirdly) of constituting such plans for the preservation and due repair of the said Stone of Scone as from time...
(lastly) of ordaining whomsoever they require for promoting Our Royal Will with greater efficacy. Given at Our...
elfth day of November in the year One thousand nine hundred and Ninety Six and in the Forty Fifth year of Our R...

PER·SIGNATURAM·MANU·S.D.N.·REGINAE·SUPRA·SCRIPTAM

THE ROYAL CASTLE
OF EDINBURGH.
ANCIENT HOME OF
THE HONOURS OF
SCOTLAND

REV. CANON DR. DONALD GRAY (LEFT)
AND THE VERY REV. MICHAEL MAYNE,
KCVO, FORMER DEAN OF WESTMINSTER
(CENTRE), EXAMINE THE STONE WITH
RICHARD WELANDER, HISTORIC
SCOTLAND'S CONSERVATOR.

The consultation process was launched on 16 July, when a consultation paper was issued by The Scottish Office to a wide range of organisations and individuals and also made available to the general public for comment. The principal criteria in deciding where the Stone should be put on display were that the location should be historic, dignified, solemn, secure and accessible to large numbers of visitors. The paper also specifically raised the question of whether the Stone should be housed in a building set aside for religious purposes. The consultation process sparked off a lively debate in Scotland and bids were made for a variety of sites which had some association with the Stone, including Scone, Dunfermline, Stirling and Arbroath. There was no strength of support for a specifically religious building.

Edinburgh Castle, and more specifically the Crown Room, emerged as the location favoured by the largest number of individuals responding to the consultation and it met the criteria. On 21 October the Government announced that The Queen had agreed that when the Stone of Destiny was returned to Scotland, it should be housed in the Crown Room alongside the Honours of Scotland. It was also announced that plans were being made to move the Stone of Destiny to Scotland so that it could be installed in Edinburgh Castle on St Andrew's Day (30 November).

The task of lifting the Stone from the Coronation Chair, packing it, transporting it back to Scotland, carrying out any necessary conservation work, and preparing it for display was to be carried out by technical experts in Historic Scotland. This was a sensitive and delicate task which would be highly visible given the world-wide publicity surrounding the return of the Stone. Meticulous planning went into the operation, including several visits to Westminster Abbey, the design and construction of a hand barrow on which to carry the Stone, and the carving of a replica with which to practise carrying it. Special measures were planned to protect both the Stone and the Coronation Chair.

On the night of 13 November the Stone was lifted out of the Coronation Chair. It had been repaired in 1951 and was therefore presumed to be fragile. It was also known that it fitted tightly into the Coronation Chair. Great care was taken to plan the lifting of the Stone, which weighs 152 kg (336 lb) in a way which would damage neither the Stone itself nor the Chair. The operation took about five hours and involved the erection of a temporary scaffolding over the Coronation Chair and the use of a block and tackle to lift the Stone with woven nylon straps. The Stone was then lowered on to the hand barrow which was covered by a fitted wooden box and sealed. It was carried out of the Abbey the following morning by a team of four from Historic Scotland, with the Dean and Chapter of Westminster in attendance. The Stone was brought north under police escort and, after one overnight stop, arrived on the English side of Coldstream Bridge on the morning of 15 November.

THE STONE CROSSING COLDSTREAM BRIDGE ON
15 NOVEMBER 1996.

Coldstream Bridge was the natural choice
as the point where the Stone should re-enter
Scotland publicly for the first time in 700
years. The bridge spans the River Tweed
and carries one of the major historic routes
between Scotland and England. The Stone,
transferred overnight to an army Land
Rover, was escorted on to Coldstream
Bridge by men of the Coldstream Guards.
It was met at the middle of the bridge by the
Secretary of State for Scotland and the Lord
Lieutenant of Berwickshire, and a new
escort, drawn from the Royal Scots and the
King's Own Scottish Borderers, took over.
In recognition of the non-political nature of
the ceremony, representatives of all the main
political parties took part. The Stone was
carried in procession behind a military brass
and pipe band through crowds of spectators
to the former Town House.

THE BRIDGE OVER THE RIVER TWEED
AT COLDSTREAM.

Following the ceremony at Coldstream, the Stone was taken to Historic Scotland's Conservation Centre in Edinburgh for conservation analysis and treatment. There it was removed from its protective packing and found to have survived its 400-mile journey without any damage. This was the first opportunity to study the Stone closely.

HISTORIC SCOTLAND'S CONSERVATORS
EXAMINE THE STONE.

In parallel with the decision-making process on the new home for the Stone in Scotland and its return to Scotland for conservation and display, planning had been underway for what was to be the most spectacular and historic day of pageantry in Scotland since The Queen's Coronation year of 1953. The planning fell largely to The Scottish Office (including Historic Scotland), the Lyon Court, the Armed Forces and the Minister and Session of St Giles' Cathedral. The aim was to organise the ceremonies surrounding the installation of the Stone in Edinburgh Castle on St Andrew's Day. This date was chosen as the most appropriate in the calendar – St Andrew is Scotland's patron saint and his cross, white on a blue background, is the national flag. Prince Andrew, His Royal Highness The Duke of York, represented Her Majesty The Queen at the ceremonies.

THE STONE ENTERS EDINBURGH CASTLE ON ST ANDREW'S DAY 1996.

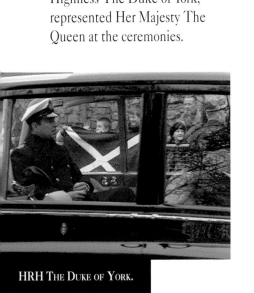

HRH THE DUKE OF YORK.

At 10.30 am on 30 November 1996 the Stone, open to public view, was transported in a specially adapted army Land Rover from the Palace of Holyroodhouse up the Royal Mile to St Giles' Cathedral. At the head of the procession of eight vehicles were mounted escorts, provided by Lothian and Borders Police and the Royal Scots Dragoon Guards, and the band of the Royal Marines. The procession was escorted by members of The Queen's Bodyguard for Scotland (Royal Company of Archers) in their highly distinctive uniforms. Among those in the procession were His Royal Highness The Duke of York, the Secretary of State for Scotland, the other Commissioners of the Regalia, the Lord Lyon King of Arms, the Lord High Constable of Scotland, Gold Stick for Scotland, and the Hereditary Bearers of the Royal Banner of Scotland (the 'Lion Rampant') and the Scottish national flag (the 'Saltire'). The day was cold but bright and sunny and an estimated 10,000 people had turned out to watch.

was carried into the Cathedral by a bearer party provided by the 1st Battalion the King's Own Scottish Borderers and escorted by Officers of the Royal Company of Archers, and placed in the Sanctuary for the duration of the service.

The Cathedral was filled with a congregation broadly representative of public life in Scotland for a 'National Service on the occasion of the return of the Stone of Destiny to Scotland'. The service, conducted by the Minister of St Giles' Cathedral, laid stress on Scotland's sense of history but also her diversity, her evolution, her place in the modern world and her future. The readings were given by ten young people from schools in Edinburgh, Glasgow, Dumfries, Eyemouth, Fraserburgh and Gairloch. The Old Testament lesson, read in Gaelic, recalled the legend of Jacob and his pillow of stone (Genesis 28, 10–22). The New Testament lesson, read in the Doric, covered the calling of Saint Andrew as a disciple and his brother Simon Peter, the rock or stone (St John 1, 35–42). The thoughtful and forward-looking tone of the service is well summed up by this short prayer, recorded in the order of service:

we offer now our prayer that people with much history may also be a people of great hope; that those who live in Scotland now may sense that they belong, no matter where their forebears lived; and each may have the opportunity of sharing the great honour of turning Scotland's past into Scotland's best tomorrow.

When the procession reached St Giles', the Stone was carried into the east end of the Cathedral. At the West Door His Royal Highness The Duke of York inspected a Guard of Honour formed by the 1st Battalion the Argyll and Sutherland Highlanders and the Highland Band of the Scottish Division. At 11 am the Ecclesiastical Procession entered the Cathedral, followed immediately by the Royal Procession. As the Royal Procession entered, a fanfare was sounded by Her Majesty's Household Trumpeters in Scotland, the rich sounds of which complemented the brilliantly coloured tabards of the members of the Lyon Court – the Carrick Pursuivant, the Kintyre Pursuivant, the Ross Herald, the Rothesay Herald, the Albany Herald, and the Lord Lyon King of Arms. When the Duke of York had taken his place in the Royal Pew, the Stone of Destiny

At the end of the service the Stone of Destiny was returned to its vehicle and the procession, now led by the Highland Band of the Scottish Division, re-formed outside the Cathedral. Then began the final stage of its journey, up the Lawnmarket, Castle Hill and the Esplanade to Edinburgh Castle.

THE STONE OF DESTINY AND THE
HONOURS OF SCOTLAND DISPLAYED TOGETHER IN
THE CROWN ROOM AT EDINBURGH CASTLE.

HRH THE DUKE OF
YORK PLACES THE
STONE IN THE SAFE
KEEPING OF THE
COMMISSIONERS OF THE
REGALIA AT A
CEREMONY IN THE
GREAT HALL OF
EDINBURGH CASTLE.

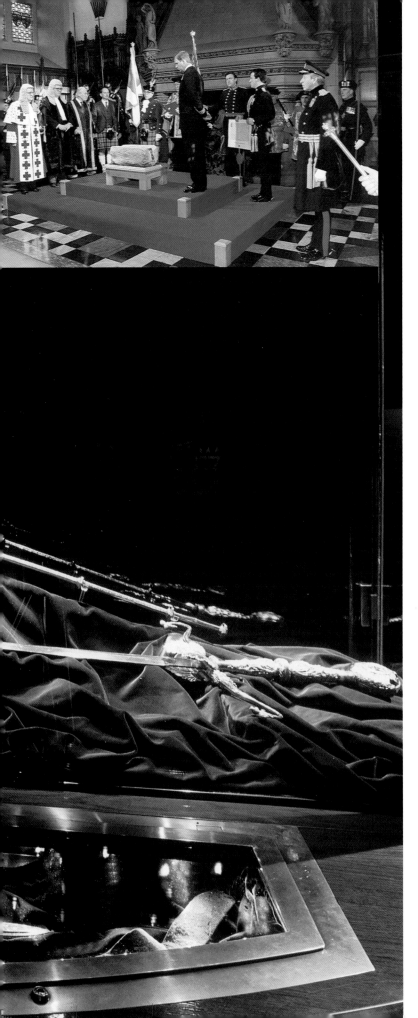

The main ceremony took place in the presence of invited guests in the Great Hall, where the Stone had been laid on a red carpeted dais. The Lord Lyon King of Arms read out the terms of the Royal Warrant entrusting the Stone of Destiny to the four Commissioners of the Regalia (the Keeper of the Great Seal, who is always the First Minister for Scotland of the day; the Lord Clerk Register; the Lord Advocate and the Lord Justice Clerk). His Royal Highness made a short speech, then handed over the Royal Warrant to the Commissioners. The Keeper of the Great Seal replied. Following this ceremony a gun salute was fired from Edinburgh Castle and returned from *HMS Newcastle*, anchored off the Port of Leith.

That night the Stone was moved from the Great Hall to the Crown Room where it was placed alongside the Honours of Scotland. There it now lies on public display in the heart of Scotland's historic capital, in the very room which James VI had had built in 1617 to house the treasures of his Scottish kingdom on the occasion of his own homecoming. When Edward I took the Stone of Destiny from Scotland in 1296 he also took the crown and sceptre of the day; while these have long since disappeared it is surely fitting that the Stone should be united with the present Honours of Scotland, the oldest set of Regalia in Europe. When Edward took the Stone, the crown, the sceptre, the Black Rood, Scotland's archives and other treasures, he hoped to crush Scotland's sense of identity and its very being. That he failed to do so can be well attested by the words of the Moderator of the General Assembly of the Church of Scotland in his address at the National Service in St Giles' Cathedral on St Andrew's Day when he reflected that:

...during all the long pilgrimage of the years, the ideal of Scottish nationhood and the reality of Scottish identity have never been wholly obliterated from the hearts of the people. The recovery of this ancient symbol of the Stone cannot but strengthen the proud distinctiveness of the people of Scotland. It will in addition bear a silent and steady witness to the mutuality of interest between those who govern and those who are governed, united in the task of promoting the welfare of the land and the destination of its people.

THE STONE OF DESTINY

'A large stone on which the Kings of Scots sat to be crowned'

The Stone of Destiny measures
570 by 420 by 265 mm (26³/₈ x 16¹/₂ x 10³/₈ in)
and weighs 152 kg (336 lb). Each end face contains an
iron staple connected to an iron ring by a figure-of-eight link. It is
formed from a coarse-grained, pinkish-buff sandstone very similar to
sandstones of the Lower Old Red Sandstone age. This stone is found
in Perthshire and Angus, indeed within a few miles of Scone. It
would be entirely possible therefore for the Stone to have been
quarried near to Scone and for it not to have been brought there from
elsewhere. Deposits of this type of rock are found elsewhere in
Scotland but not in sufficiently large deposits to allow the quarrying
of such a substantial block. It has been suggested that the Stone is a
cut-down Roman altar, but it bears no evidence to support this

The sides are roughly dressed, probably with a chisel and certainly with a punch, but not all to the same standard. The upper half of the Stone is much better dressed than the bottom, which is also broken away at the corners. We cannot be certain when this damage occurred, but it may suggest that only the top part of the Stone was intended to be seen, with the sides obscured from view.

The top surface of the Stone shows evidence for many actions. Immediately obvious is the 'rectangle' cut into the surface. This gives the appearance of having been roughly, indeed hastily, executed. It also shows evidence for two different hands at work. The original mason had a reasonable degree of skill, but the task was finished in a much cruder manner by an unskilled person. At the left-hand side, a second groove was cut, probably later. The purpose of this rectangle is not known. Its rough state suggests that the task was never completed, perhaps abandoned when it was realised the Stone was cracked and might fracture if work continued. It is possible that the intention was to create a receptacle, perhaps for a cushion or to house a holy relic. Two crosses were cut into the top of the stone, one towards the right-hand corner, the other

The scoops in the ends of the Stone were cut after the rectangle. They were clearly cut to hold the iron rings which were connected to the Stone by iron staples: the staples were held in place by lead run into the holes in the Stone. Later, the staples were shaved on their outer edges. It was certainly after the cutting of the rectangle, and almost certainly after the sinking for the rings, that the surface of the Stone was smoothed, for the edges of the rectangle and of the cuts for the iron rings are not sharp. The smoothing could have been done with another stone, but the wear could also have been caused by other action, such as walking on the Stone.

As the cutting of the scoops for the iron rings is demonstrably not the last action to the Stone, it seems unlikely that these were cut to aid its removal to London in 1296. The Stone had to be moved out of the abbey church of Scone for the inauguration of the kings, so it is possible that the rings were inserted to help on these occasions. However, the thinning of the iron staples could have occurred as a result of its removal to London. The thinning seriously weakened the staples and is unlikely to have taken place if it was intended to continue to use them. The simplest explanation is that Walter the Painter had been given the measurements of the Stone to enable him to make the chair, but his information did not include mention of the rings. Thus the staples might have been thinned to allow insertion of the Stone into the chair

We have few contemporary medieval descriptions of the Stone. In the inventory of royal jewels made in 1296, the Stone is described as 'a large stone on which the Kings of

Scots sat to be crowned'. Fordun described it as: 'a stone cut out of marble in the form of a chair', and Walter of Guisborough similarly as: 'a very large stone, hollowed out and partly fashioned in the form of a round chair'. This sounds more like a bishop's throne such as survives at Hexham: perhaps Walter had been informed that the throne was stone and thought it would be like the bishops' thrones with which he was familiar. We should not place too much credence in the statement that the Stone was marble: as late as 1874 it was described as limestone, when it is clearly sandstone.

Walter of Guisborough stated that the Stone was kept beside the high altar in the abbey church of Scone, founded by Alexander I soon after 1120; where the Stone was lodged earlier is not known. Nor is it known whether the Kings of Scots were inaugurated sitting directly on the Stone or whether it was encased in a throne. Fordun wrote of 'a chair – that is, the stone', William Rishanger of 'the regal stone' and Walter of Guisgborough of 'the Coronation Chair'. We have no idea what that chair would have looked like. The Great Seals of the Kings of Scots illustrate various types of thrones and, although it is unlikely that they depict the actual inauguration throne, they do indicate the range of possibilities and perhaps give support to the theory that by 1296 the Stone was enclosed in a wooden chair. The seals of kings for 150 years from Edgar to Alexander II (about 1100 to 1250) show them seated on stools of various forms of elaboration. Fashions then changed and the seals of Alexander III and John Balliol both show wooden chairs with high backs. Let us leave the last word to Fordun, who described it as 'a marble chair, sculptured in very antique workmanship by a careful artist'. As this description does not fit the Stone in any particular, perhaps he was describing the chair in which it rested.

THE SEAL OF ALEXANDER III SHOWING HIM SEATED ON AN ELABORATE THRONE.

Clickhimin

SHETLAND

Kirkwall

ORKNEY

THE
NORTH
SEA

SCOTLAND

Arbroath

Iona

Dunstaffnage

Scone

Dunadd

Stirling

Forth

Dunfermline

Dunbar

Clyde

Edinburgh

Berwick
~upon~Tweed

Norham

Tweed

Coldstream

THE
IRISH
SEA

A MAP OF SCOTLAND INDICATING SOME OF
THE PLACES MENTIONED IN THE BOOK.

47

THE AUTHORS, GRAEME MUNRO (LEFT) AND DAVID BREEZE
(THIRD FROM THE LEFT), EXAMINE THE STONE.